The Cooperative Program and the Road to Serfdom
By G. Seth Dunn, MAcc, MDiv, CPA

This work is dedicated to faithful givers everywhere.

FOREWORD

Baptist born, Baptist bred, and when I die, I'll be a Baptist dead. That's me. That's who I've always been.

Saved in a Southern Baptist church, baptized in a Southern Baptist church, licensed to preach in a Southern Baptist church, graduating from a Southern Baptist school, having planted Southern Baptist churches, pastoring Southern Baptist churches, I am a Southern Baptist. Heritage means so much to a person like me. And frankly, so does loyalty. I'm a native Southerner. We don't give up easily and we are slow to back off of our traditions.

I knew who Lottie Moon was before I knew who Santa Claus was. I collected my dimes and nickels for Annie Armstrong as a child. I've been on mission in cooperation with the IMB. I've been on mission in cooperation with NAMB and my state convention. I've received financial support from NAMB and other SBC entities to do my work. I've been on the blessed receiving end of Cooperative Program dollars, and that money has helped me in times past to purchase a church van, renovate a church building in one of our local missions, and helped stock the food in our church pantry. I get the value, because I have received it personally in monetary form.

And then, something changed a number of years ago. I began to see the state convention give money - with strings attached - in exchange for a promise of loyalty to the state director. I saw numbers fudged – and in fact, *fabricated* – by our local association and state convention. I saw *incredible* waste of funds by NAMB and our state convention. When the Great Commission Resurgence Taskforce Report forced restructuring of my state convention to eliminate unnecessary personnel, I saw female employees of the Convention be "let go," only to be put into new positions as church planters. And in trying to seek clarity on some of these matters, I've seen both NAMB and the state convention act retributively against those of us who dared to question them. The list of ways that I've seen Cooperative Program funds be abused goes on forever, and far outweighs the money that is actually received on the field.

Asking people to rethink giving – or how they give – to the Cooperative Program makes me feel like a bit of a Judas. Not only have I been paying into the pot my entire life, I've taken from the pot. And yet, I'll always remember a check being handed to me over the table of the Montana State Convention director's office and as I grabbed the corner, he held on to his corner as well, saying "...*with this, you understand, comes a few strings.*"

Several weeks ago, a NAMB missionary wrote to me to tell his account of publicly disagreeing on his Facebook page with IMB president, David Platt's, reversal of a policy that would now allow private tongue-speakers to serve in foreign missions. He was contacted by NAMB and told to remove his social media post, or face consequences. Cooperative Program giving has, in effect, become hush money. Dolling out Cooperative Program funds has so often mimicked the strategy of left-wing Washington politicians – it is a means to control, to silence, and to earn favors. And like a government bureaucracy, the more people who are on the dole, the more people owe the system. It is, essentially, paid loyalty.

And then came the day I read *Spending God's Money* by Mary Kinney Branson. Branson was the highest-ranking woman in NAMB's history and detailed the extreme financial management at the entity. Her details, citations, and facts seem indisputable, as NAMB's president resigned with a five hundred thousand dollar severance package and a PR firm was paid with Cooperative Program dollars to rebuild his reputation. How did NAMB respond to claims of purchasing ice sculptures for parties, staff retreats in the islands and the giving out sweet no-bid kick-back deals to some of Southern Baptists' greatest celebrities? Was it with a thoughtful and sound negation? Did they provide any counterpoints or clarification? No. NAMB responded with a press release saying simply that "there are two sides to every story." To this day, NAMB has not come clean with us – chiefly because they don't have to. Trustees are not held into account, and speaking out against NAMB or its financial waste is treated as though tantamount to speaking out against Jesus Himself.

Fast-forward a few years. We have seen a Muslim enrolled at Southwestern Baptist seminary as (supposedly) an "evangelism opportunity" and instead of rebuking the seminary president, Paige Patterson, for breaking the bylaws and acting in opposition of the seminary's charter, the seminary's trustees changed the official policy to make more such "exceptions" possible. When Patterson said he would break the rules all over again if he had it to do over at the 2014 Convention, he received wild applause. We've seen the Ethics and Religious Liberty Commission president, Russell Moore, claim Jesus was an illegal alien and opined on why it would be ethical to attend a gay wedding celebration. Another seminary president, Danny Akin, of Southeastern Baptist Theological Seminary, has partnered and endorsed *Openly Secular*, an organization founded in part by atheist, Richard Dawkins, because we can cooperate with them – Akin says - on things like "poverty and creation care." Lifeway, an entity of the SBC, sells practically every heresy under the sun upon their shelves – from modalist heretics to prophets claiming direct and divine revelation to prosperity gospel preachers. And the books they don't set on the shelves, like Joel Osteen's or Joyce Meyer's, they'll happily order for you. Emails have been released demonstrating that Lifeway executives Ed Stetzer and Thom Rainer were told that the Heaven Tourism book, *The Boy Who Came Back From Heaven*, was fabricated (told to them by a former Lifeway trustee, no less) and chose to continue to sell the book until international media attention made it too problematic. Lifeway spokesman, Marty King, claimed that Lifeway only became aware of the book's fabrication with recent media attention, which is demonstrably, factually, ridiculously untrue. In short, our entities have been behaving very, very badly. Trustee positions are given intentionally to those perceived to challenge the system the least, and so the system perpetuates itself.

How are we to support any of this? How are we pastors to look into the eyes of our people and tell them that giving to the Cooperative Program (at least as we're currently doing it) is going to be money well spent and well stewarded? For many of us, giving to the Cooperative Program is just something we do as Southern Baptists. And yet, that tradition must not let us turn faithful cooperation into a golden cow that can't be toppled.

As Baptists, we cooperate. Cooperation is our DNA. What Seth has presented in this small book are a list of ways that we can cooperate without throwing our dollars away as poor stewards, along with a thorough analysis of how Cooperative Program funds are terribly abused and ineffective. As an accountant and a Southern Baptist, Seth is uniquely positioned to give a thoroughly economic understanding of the Cooperative Program and why we need to rethink how we go about our financial partnerships.

Please read it. Please share it. Grace and Peace to you, the reader...

JD Hall
June 2015
Pastor, Fellowship Baptist Church (SBC)
President, Reformation Montana

PREFACE TO THE 1ST EDITION

I was saved in a Baptist Church. I attended VBS in Southern Baptist Churches. I was baptized in a Baptist church. I married a Baptist. I attend a Baptist seminary.

I am a Baptist of Baptists.

Though it was not done on the *eighth* day, I was dedicated at Woodland Park Baptist Church soon after my birth. I grew up attending that Southern Baptist church on Sunday mornings as a part of a family that faithfully gave. As a carefree middle-class youth, I never knew how much was given, but it made an impression on me every week to see my father put a check in the offering plate. He modeled something to me - the importance of giving. Giving matters. So, too, does stewardship. The Cooperative Program of the Southern Baptist Convention, to which so many Baptists give, is funded by giving and administered by stewards. It deserves then, thorough, investigation.

I grew up at an elder-led church that directly supported missionaries and featured expository preaching from the pulpit. (We also had the two best church softball teams in East Chattanooga.) It was (and still is) a part of the Southern Baptist Convention but it was independent-minded church. During the liberal days of the Southern Baptist Theological Seminary, the pastor had a negative experience attending class there which I believe colored his view of the convention as a whole. The Cooperative Program wasn't pushed in the congregation. When I was little, I didn't know how blessed I was to grow up in a church like that. I now do.

I first learned about the Cooperative Program when I enrolled in a seminary in my mid-twenties. Coming from a business background (I'm a CPA with two business degrees), the Cooperative Program seemed inefficient to me. It seemed a little outmoded and a little too bureaucratic but it didn't seem like a big problem. However, the more I learned about the convention and the more I read about economics, the less I supported the Cooperative Program. I may be cutting off my nose to spite my face here, since the Cooperative Program subsidizes my tuition, but I think giving through the Cooperative Program is a really bad idea. I think it should be stopped.

There are a lot of good-hearted people who will disagree with me. Further, there are a lot of good-hearted, kingdom-minded people who support their families on salaries funded by the Cooperative Program. My position is a tough one to take. However, I take it still. I see too much mismanagement and controversy to take another. Not everyone will see controversy where I see it. There is room for polite and sincere disagreement. Yet, I'm arguing against a central planning system itself, not necessarily all of the results (some good, some bad) it has produced. If church leaders and every day pew-sitting Baptists apply the economic sense they use in their political and business affairs, I believe, they will see the Cooperative Program how I see it. In *The Cooperative Program and the Road to Serfdom*, I make a bold argument. It is one, I believe, that I support with facts. I hope you'll consider it.

G. Seth Dunn
June 2015

PREFACE TO THE 2nd EDITION

The first edition of *The Cooperative Program and the Road to Serfdom* was released as an e-book three years ago. It was always my intention to publish this work in a paperback format, updating its contents along the way. Raising a family, my career, and completing seminary have prevented me from doing so. Now, having completed my Masters of Divinity from the New Orleans Baptist Theological Seminary, in the wake of the unceremonious dismissal of Conservative Resurgence hero Paige Patterson from Southwestern Baptist Theological Seminary and what seems like an onslaught of progressive influence in the SBC, I find myself compelled to finish my original project.

In the 1st Edition, I intentionally steered clear of criticizing the International Mission Board (IMB). An urgency to engage in foreign missions spurred the creation of the Southern Baptist Convention and I did not want any criticism of the Convention's "one sacred effort" to share the gospel across the globe to deter readers from considering my proposal to abandon the Cooperative Program as a mechanism of funding. However, since the publication of the 1st Edition, a multi-million-dollar budget deficit in IMB operations has come to light. Such gross financial mismanagement in the most important Southern Baptist agency cannot be ignored. Thus, the 2nd Edition includes a section about poor stewardship practices in the IMB. To be certain, there are grave theological matters in the SBC which are not covered in this book (Things have gotten so bad in the convention that JD Hall, the long-time Southern Baptist pastor who wrote the foreword to this book has led his church to leave the convention). I write about these matters often at Pulpit & Pen (pulpitandpen.org) and discuss them regularly on my podcast, the Christian Commute

(Christiancommute.podomatic.com). Where this work is concerned, it is my hope that readers of this book will focus on wise financial stewardship and reconsider their participation in the Cooperative Program.

G. Seth Dunn
June 2018

Reconsidering the Cooperative Program

The Southern Baptist Convention (SBC) is the one of the largest Christian denominations in the world[1]; it is one which holds a biblically sound statement of faith.[2] The SBC is known far and wide for its emphasis on evangelical mission work and biblically conservative stance on social issues. Though the SBC is widely-known, many people know very little about its operations: how it is organized, how it is led, and how it is funded. For example, many Southern Baptists might be surprised to find out that the Southern Baptist Convention has no assets, no employees, owns no property, and only exists for two days a year.[3]

The Southern Baptist Convention itself is a yearly gathering of independent member churches. During this annual gathering (called a "convention"), member church representatives elect leaders to administer Southern Baptist causes on a day-to-day basis. These causes, which operate throughout year, are funded through the voluntary giving of independent member churches. The lion's share of this funding comes through what is known as "Cooperative Program" giving. The Cooperative Program has served to fund Southern Baptist operations since 1925.[4] Unfortunately, the Cooperative Program is outmoded. To make matters worse, Cooperative Program monies are being used to fund initiatives, at a national level, that many Southern Baptist laypeople would find objectionable if they

---

[1] Southern Baptists claimed a membership of 16,267,494 affiliated with 43,465 in 2004, according to Brand and Hankins

[2] I refer to the Baptist Faith and Message 2000

[3] Brand, C. O. (2009). *One Sacred Effort: The Cooperative Program of Southern Baptists.* B&H Academic. p. 100

[4] ibid p. 112

only knew about them. Cooperative Program giving arguably supports what has become a top-heavy, bureaucratic, politically-motivated, money-centered religiopolitical empire that is operated by a class of clerical elites who do not represent Southern Baptist interests at a grass roots label. A number of factors, the chief of which may be ignorance, allow the situation to persist. The existence of this problem situation calls for a review of the history of the Cooperative Program, a survey of Southern Baptist entities, an analysis of the economic effectiveness and efficiency of the Cooperative Program, a biblical reflection on Southern Baptist Stewardship and ecclesiology, and, most importantly, a solution and call to action. The solution and call to action are both simple and locally-focused: local churches should support their preferred Southern Baptist denominational causes, if any, by giving around the Cooperative Program and directly to Southern Baptist entities and missionaries.

A New Deal: The Birth of the Cooperative Program

"What the Hoover Dam became to agriculture and industry in the southwestern United States, the Cooperative Program would become to Southern Baptists. The same superlative evaluation made by President Roosevelt concerning the Hoover Dam is fitting for the Cooperative Program."[5] Chad Owen Brand and David Hankins

"...people who are concerned about the economy need to take a closer look at history. We deserve something better than repeating the 1930s disasters...No matter how much worse things got after government intervention under Roosevelt's New Deal policies, the party line was that he had to 'do something' to get us out of the disaster created by the failure of the unregulated market" [6] Thomas Sowell

The Southern Baptist Convention was created in 1845 for the purpose of "organizing a plan for eliciting, combining, and directing the energies of the whole (Baptist) denomination in one sacred effort for the propagation of the gospel."[7] This effort would require funding. Until 1925, the Southern Baptist Convention largely financed its denominational enterprises through boots-on-the-ground

---

[5] ibid p.3

[6] Sowell, T. (2008, December 23). *Another Great Depression?*. Retrieved November 2014, 30, from NationalReview.com: http://www.nationalreview.com/articles/226599/another-great-depression/thomas-sowell/page/0/1

[7] Baptist Studies Online. (2007, February). *Original Constitution of the Southern Baptist Convention.* Retrieved November 30, 2014, from http://baptiststudiesonline.com/: http://baptiststudiesonline.com/wp-content/uploads/2007/02/constitution-of-the-sbc.pdf

fundraising efforts. The representatives of these denominational enterprises would hit the road, like old-time Methodist circuit riders, and solicit individual SBC churches for financial support. "Sunday by Sunday, fundraisers from seminaries and colleges, orphanages and hospitals, mission boards and benevolent organizations fanned out among the churches asking the faithful for help…the costs of raising the money sometimes approached 50 percent of the proceeds…churches were beleaguered by an endless stream of denominational representatives needing 'pulpit time' to make their appeals."[8] For example, a representative from the Foreign Mission board might solicit funds from a church in June. In July, a representative from a seminary might solicit funds from the same church. The mission board representative, by virtue of his earlier arrival, might receive more giving. Conversely, the seminary representative might receive more giving by virtue of a superior speaking ability. Such potentialities resulted in an unequal distribution of denominational giving. "The more popular, or perhaps the swifter, received a disproportionate share of the earnings."[9] In order to ensure a more even distribution of denominational giving, the Cooperative Program was created. The Cooperative Program created a central source of funding for SBC enterprises. To do so, it became a central recipient of giving. In a sense, the Cooperative Program was created to spread the wealth.

In their book, *One Sacred Effort: The Cooperative Program and Southern Baptists*, authors Chad Owen Brand and David E. Hankins liken the inception of the Cooperative Program in the 1920s to another "visionary

---

[8] Brand, C. O. (2009). *One Sacred Effort: The Cooperative Program of Southern Baptists*. B&H Academic p. 2-3
[9] ibid p. 2

plan"[10] plan of the Progressive Era. This "visionary" plan was that of the construction of the Hoover Dam. "(The) Hoover Dam was just the first prominent example of the state-directed and state-funded industrialization of the Pacific states...bringing the Far West much closer to the industrial policy of pre-and postwar Japan and rather distant from 'the natural workings of the market.'"[11] Upon his first glimpse of the Hoover Damn, English novelist J.B. Priestly remarked, "Here is the soul of American under socialism"[12] The Hoover Dam, the construction of which was begun under the administration of Hebert Hoover and completed under that of Franklin Delano Roosevelt, epitomizes New Deal-era progressive socialism. The analogy drawn by Brand and Hankins between the Cooperative Program and the Hoover Dam, then, is an appropriate one because so, too, does the Cooperative Program. The Cooperative Program, like the New Deal, is a product of 1920s-era centrally planned progressivism. It collects wealth from a large body and puts it under the control of central decision makers, who presumably know how best how to redistribute it. The progressive nature of their denominational financing program may seem surprising to modern-era Southern Baptists who are generally associated with conservative, free-market republican or libertarian leanings.[13] However, progressive democrats dominated the Political landscape of the southern United States (which was and is Southern Baptist

---

[10] ibid p. 1

[11] Cumings, B. (2009). *Dominion from Sea to Sea: Pacific Ascendancy and American Power.* Yale University Press p. 259

[12] ibid

[13] See Appendix 1. For more information see "How the Faithful Voted" at the Pew Forum website.

country) during the Progressive Era.[14] In keeping with progressive thought, Southern Baptists of the time rejected the soliciting of funds by individual entities at individual churches in favor of a centralized means of collecting and spending (the Cooperative Program) managed by top-level bureaucrats.

---

[14] See Appendix 2. States in which the Democratic Candidate prevailed are show in blue.

Funding SBC Entities

"I believe in the Cooperative Program because it is the best means of mission support in the world." Don Hattaway, *Georgia Baptist Convention President*[15]

"While Central Planning may no longer be a credible form of economic organization, it is clear that the intellectual battle for its rival-free market capitalism and globalization- is far from won." Alan Greenspan[16]

"For years, (the Cooperative Program) made it possible for small churches to be a part of sending missionaries to distant countries and obscure parts of the United States...With improved communication, transportation, and technology, today's small churches can easily be involved in mission causes around the world...the Cooperative Program now supports astronomical salaries for agency CEOs, maintenance of huge agency office buildings, and programs that are duplicated in state conventions, associations, and local churches."[17] Even though local churches no longer need the Cooperative Program to participate in world missions, many still fund it. In doing so, they place their dollars in the hands of an oligarchy of elite power brokers. "These leaders - some estimate their number to be about 35 - make many SBC decisions in restaurants and motel rooms long before motions are

---

[15] Georgia Bapist Convention. (2013). *We Believe In the Cooperative Program*. Retrieved May 22, 2015, from Georgia Bapist Convention: http://gabaptist.org/we-believe-in-cp/

[16] Greenspan, A. (2008). *The Age of Turbulence: Adventures in a New World*. Penguin p. 267

[17] Branson, M. K. (2007). *Spending God's Money: Extravagance and Misuse in the Name of Ministry*. Lee's Summit, MO: Father's Press, LLC p. 15-16

officially made on the floor of the annual Convention. This small group of powerful leaders are the ones spending the money for more than 16 million Southern Baptists."[18] These elite central planners distribute Cooperative Program money that the SBC receives to four of six primary Southern Baptist causes: The International Mission Board, The North American Mission Board, six Southern Baptist Seminaries, and The Ethics and Religious Liberty Commission. The remaining two causes, LifeWay Christian Resources and Guidestone Financial Resources are self-supporting.

The International Mission Board

The International Mission Board (IMB) employs a force of thousands of missionaries all around the world. As of 2004, "the number of missionaries was approaching 5,300. These missionaries and overseas groups they work with started 21,000 new churches and baptized 600,000 in 2004. The total 2004 budget of the IMB was $242,526,532[19]. Cooperative Program support provides about 35% of this budget while the Lottie Moon Christmas Offering for International Missions provides about 55 percent."[20] The 2015 IMB budget was $301,100,000.[21] As of May 13,

---

[18] ibid p. 17

[19] Adjusted by the Consumer Price Index, this amount of money is worth 307,060,000 in 2015 dollars. This means that the IMB budget has outpaced inflation while reducing its headcount of field missionaries since 2004. I used the following online calculator to perform CPI calculations: https://www.minneapolisfed.org/

[20] Brand, C. O. (2009). *One Sacred Effort: The Cooperative Program of Southern Baptists*. B&H Academic p.141

[21] IMB. (2015). *Fast facts*. Retrieved May 28, 2015, from www.imb.org: http://www.imb.org/1307.aspx#.VWer0PlVhBc

2015, there were 4,743 missionaries on the field.[22] IMB missionaries are expected to affirm the confession of faith of the Southern Baptist Convention.

The North American Mission Board

"Most Southern Baptists are completely clueless about how their denomination has supported its domestic mission efforts in the decades since World War II. This ignorance is not limited to the average layperson in the pew but is shared by most pastors as well…This reflects a widespread failure on the part of Southern Baptist leaders at the national, state, association, and local church levels to do meaningful missions and stewardship education…" Glen A Land[23]

The North American Mission (NAMB) board is the domestic counterpart of the International Mission Board. "In conjunction with the Baptist state conventions, NAMB supports approximately five thousand missionaries in North America. These missionaries are involved in numerous assignments such as church planting, chaplaincy, resort missions, social ministries, and so forth. Southern Baptists, under the NAMB's strategy, have been starting approximately seventeen hundred new churches a year for the last several years. The 2004 budget was $118,285,000. The Cooperative Program provided more than 36 percent of that total while the Annie Armstrong Easter Offering for

---

[22] ibid

[23] http://baptistbanner.org/Subarchive_4/410%20GCRTF%20Glen%20Land.htm

North American Missions provided 43 percent."[24] The 2015 NAMB budget was $121,550,000.[25]

Seminaries

There are six Southern Baptist seminaries. They are located in California, Missouri, Louisiana, North Carolina, Kentucky, and Texas. They vary in size and enrollment. "The six seminaries educated over fifteen thousand different students in 2003-04 at a cost of about $110,000,000. The Southern Baptist Cooperative Program provided over $40,000,000 to this cause."[26] Southern Baptist seminaries are also funded by tuition, fees, and private donations. Non-Southern Baptist students can enroll; however, instructors are expected to teach in accordance with the confession of faith of the Southern Baptist Convention.

The Ethics and Religious Liberty Commission

The Ethics and Religious Liberty Commission (ERLC) is the lobbying arm of the Southern Baptist Convention and maintains offices in Nashville and Washington, D.C. "With twenty-four staff members and a 2003-2004 CP allocations of $2,825,268…With regular print and electronic media and a daily radio broadcast, the ERLC endeavors to keep Baptists and others informed and motivated about moral, cultural, and civic concerns. The

---

[24] ibid
[25] NAMB. (2015). *2015 NORTH AMERICAN MISSION BOARD MINISTRY REPORT*. Retrieved May 28, 2015, from www.namb.net: http://www.namb.net/annualreport/
[26] Ibid p.142

total budget in 2003-2004 was $3,385,177."[27] The 2014 ERLC budget was 3,190,000.[28]

LifeWay Christian Resources & GuideStone Financial Resources

LifeWay Christian Resources and GuideStone Financial Resources are controlled by the Southern Baptist Convention but are not supported by Cooperative Program Funding. These entities are self-supporting. LifeWay Christian Resources evolved out of the Southern Baptist Sunday School Board. LifeWay "produces literature, Bible studies, training materials, conferences, music, and much more for all age groups and sizes and churches and organizations. LifeWay is a very large corporation with a budget of over $450,000,000 (2004) and around fifteen hundred employees. LifeWay Christian Resources has never received Cooperative Program funds from the Southern Baptist Convention but is self-supporting. It invests a significant amount in Southern Baptist missions and ministries worldwide."[29] Guidestone Financial Resources, formerly the "Annuity Board", provides financial and insurance services for denominational employees, seminary students, and pastors. It supports itself through the fees it charges for providing these services.

---

[27] ibid

[28] Strode, T. (2013, September 13). *TRUSTEES: ERLC budget set at $3.19M.* Retrieved May 28, 2015, from Baptist Press: http://www.bpnews.net/41089/trustees-erlc-budget-set-at-319m

[29] Brand, C. O. (2009). *One Sacred Effort: The Cooperative Program of Southern Baptists.* B&H Academic p.143

Economics, the Anointed Class, and the SBC Demographic

"On both sides of the Atlantic, it is only a little overstated to say that we preach individualism and competitive capitalism, and practice socialism." Milton Friedman

All Cooperative Program money is passed through state conventions, which take a cut of it to fund their own initiatives, before it is passed along to the national convention. For example, an SBC church in the state of Kentucky may send in $100 to the Kentucky Baptist Convention through the Cooperative Program. The Kentucky state convention would keep $50 and send the remaining $50 to the national Convention in Nashville, Tennessee.[30] Cooperative Program money passes through at least three levels of bureaucracy before it is spent: the state convention, the national convention, and the national entity. Often these bureaucracies are headed by a member of the evangelical intelligentsia who is famous among denominationally-minded pastors but largely unknown to every-day pew-sitting Southern Baptists. A bureaucratic intelligentsia distributing funds as it sees fit runs contrary to the political and economic views of most contemporary Southern Baptists, who, as Republicans and Libertarians, tend to favor local control and streamlined organizations. The divide between the economic theory that drives the Cooperative Program and the economic theory that underlies free-market conservatism may be widened by the mindset of the pastors who champion the program. Pastors who study subjects such as theology, music, and church education in bible colleges and seminaries largely do not

---

[30] I used a 50/50 split as an example. I did not confirm the actual CP distribution percentage used by the Kentucky Baptist Convention.

receive instruction that focuses on economic theory as a part of their schooling. They are, however, educated about the importance of funding the Cooperative Program, a program which in many cases subsidizes the cost of their educations.

The modern Southern Baptist Convention is essentially what Thomas Sowell might call a "Vision of the Anointed." In his book of the same name Sowell describes a class of political elites, an intelligentsia, who are under the impression that they know what is best for people of lesser wisdom and should be given the power to structure society as they see fit. This vision, the vision of the anointed,[31] is prominent in progressive democratic political circles. Strangely enough, it is also prominent in the Sothern Baptist Convention. The Anointed Class is not to be questioned. "This (liberal) vision so permeates the media and academia, and has made such major inroads into the religious community, that many grow into adulthood unaware that there is any other way of looking at things, or that: *evidence*: might be relevant to checking out the sweeping assumptions of so-called 'thinking people'. Many of these 'thinking people' could more accurately be characterized as: *articulate*: people, as people whose verbal nimbleness can elude both evidence and logic. This can be

---

[31] The technical name Sowell gives for this vision is the "unconstrained vision." Those who hold to this vision believe that an anointed class is in best position to make beneficial decisions for society. It is often associated with liberal academics and big-government progressives. The antithesis of this vision is the "constrained vision". Those who hold to this view believe that society is too complicated for an elite group to centrally plan what is best for ever. It is also associated with free-market capitalists. For more on these competing worldviews see Sowell's book *A Conflict of Visions*.

a fatal talent, when it supplies the crucial insulation from reality behind many historic catastrophes..."[32] Those who accept the vision of the anointed "are deemed to be not only factually correct but morally on a higher plane. Put differently, those who disagree with the prevailing vision are seen as not being not merely in error, but in sin."[33] Southern Baptist preachers are both articulate and highly respected among their constituencies; perhaps more so than any other group of men. Those who support the Cooperative Program and heavy denominational influence possess the verbal nimbleness to defend their vision. Dissent from every day Baptists to the vision of denominational leadership has been condemned at both the state and national level.

As the information age has made it easier to disseminate news to the masses, bloggers have become some of the most vocal and effective critics of SBC leadership. This led the Georgia Baptist Convention, in 2007, to pass a resolution condemning blogging about Baptist matters.[34] At the same time, the Georgia Convention approved a $52.3 million dollar Cooperative Program Budget. In 2015, ERLC communications specialist, Samuel Jones, admonished readers to never start a watchdog blog.[35]

---

[32] Sowell, T. (1995). *The Vision of the Annointed.* Basic Books. p.6

[33] Sowell, T. (1995). *The Vision of the Annointed.* Basic Books. p.3

[34] Elliot, H. (2007, November 27). *Georgia Baptist resolution criticizes Baptist blogs.* Retrieved May 16, 2015, from Baptist Standard Publishing: https://www.baptiststandard.com/resources/archives/47-2007-archives/7247-georgia-baptist-resolution-criticizes-baptist-blogs

[35] James, S. (2015, MAy 7). *What Not to Do When a Fellow Christian Embarrases Us.* Retrieved May 16, 2015, from

People outside of the know are encouraged to keep any objections out of the public eye, in deference to the judgment and reputation of the anointed class.

The anointed class of the SBC almost wholeheartedly endorses the Cooperative Program, which funds their own power and influence (at the expense of smaller, low-profile churches and their pastors), while completely ignoring the fact that there is a lack of economic evidence which indicates that the Cooperative Program is the best way to spend Southern Baptist money. According to the free-market, local-control-oriented worldview of the average American conservative, such a program is folly. The Cooperative Program is liberal progressivism in the hands of purportedly conservative theologians. It should not escape notice that Cooperative Program was accepted by liberal progressives for years until they were ousted from the convention during the Conservative Resurgence Era. The conservatives who took control of the convention pushed for strong doctrinal standards but maintained the liberal progressive way of funding the convention. It funds their power and influence. It funds their vision, whatever it may be.

It is becoming more and more expected of pastors in the convention to take on the role of the "vision caster" of their church. According to the Pastor Emeritus of mega-church First Baptist Houston and oft-feature NAMB speaker, John Bisagno, "The pastor must be the vision caster. This means he must have a vision to cast, which presupposes time with

---

Patheos.com:
http://www.patheos.com/blogs/inklingations/2015/05/07/what-not-to-do-when-a-fellow-christian-embarrasses-the-rest-of-us/

God to receive the vision."[36] Bisagno is but one of the Southern Baptist Convention's vaunted leadership gurus from the mega-church mold. These gurus espouse what is known as a "Moses Model"[37] of church leadership in which a pastor runs a top-down organization like a CEO rather than providing boots-on-the-ground care to members of the flock. In Pastor's Handbook (which is offered for sale at NAMB church planting courses and assigned in SBC seminary classes), Bisagno states "Pastor those who pastor others. You must give primary attention to your leaders and their families. Most church members in the hospital may get only a phone call from the pastor. The chairman of deacons gets a visit."[38] The modern mega-church pastor, supposedly anointed with a vision for the people from God, is too busy managing a large organization from the top down to provide low-level pastoral care to non-leaders. His job is to cast a vision. Another church leadership guru, Aubrey Malphurs, wrote in his book, Being Leaders: The Authentic Nature of Christian Leadership, "A vision is the future of the ministry. Far too many churches remain stuck in the past, usually twenty to thirty years behind the culture. The vision forces them to think in terms of the future. God uses it to help them see what their future could be. While we can't predict the future, the vision will…People walk away from a vision-casting session talking about what must

---

[36] Bisagno, J. R. (2011). *Pastor's Handbook n* (Kindle Edition ed.). B&H Publishing. p. 25

[37] For a more in-depth critique of the Moses Model see my article "Dismantling the Jethro Principle" at https://gsethdunn.wordpress.com/2015/03/11/dismantling-the-jethro-principal/

[38] Bisagno, J. R. (2011). *Pastor's Handbook n* (Kindle Edition ed.). B&H Publishing. p. 75

be."[39] Whatever such an esoteric vision actually is, it is clear from the Baptist leadership gurus that it is bestowed by God upon anointed CEO-type pastors and it should not be questioned.

Such leaders, divorced from the responsibility of everyday pastoral care, have a greater amount of time to manage denominational concerns. It has become expected that they should lead the Convention as a whole. Former SBC Second VP and popular Baptist blogger Dave Miller once stated in bluntly, "Let's face it folks, the job of SBC president is a mega-job. Mega-church pastors are mega-church pastors because they are wired that way. Their gifts, personality, calling – however you bill it. Maybe, somewhere there is a pastor of a small-to-medium church who is able to handle this job. But guys like that usually move up. The mega church pastors have extensive staff to keep the home-fires burning while they are out doing their denominational service. In a mega-church, the Senior Pastor is a vision-caster and idea-guy who doesn't involve himself beyond preaching Sunday and vision-casting for the church. He's less hands-on than pastors like me. So, while he's out and about he can continue some of that vision-casting (I actually hate that word!) and preaching and let his staff carry on."[40] Even medium-sized church pastors like Dave Miller are resigned the notion that the

---

[39] Malphurs, A. (2003-09-01). *Being Leaders: The Nature of Authentic Christian Leadership* (Kindle Edition ed.). Baker Publishing Group.
[40] Miller, D. (2015, May 8). *"Dave Miller for President" and Other Dumb Ideas!* Retrieved May 16, 2015, from SBCVoices.com: http://sbcvoices.com/dave-miller-for-president-and-other-dumb-ideas/

type of pastors who "moves up"[41] is the only type of pastor suitable to run the convention. Yet, these mega-church pastors are not representative of rank-and-file Southern Baptists. They are a self-appointed anointed class and this class has great influence on the next of its members to be chosen for lucrative, high-profile leadership positions.

Rarely does one of the anointed fail to take his turn leading the convention. In 2006, current SBC President Ronnie Floyd actually lost an election after being nominated by former President and fellow megapastor, Johnny Hunt. "Johnny Hunt nominated Floyd in 2006, stating that he was convinced that Ronnie Floyd was 'the man God raised up" for the job.' God must have disagreed with Johnny Hunt; Floyd was soundly defeated by Frank Page. As it turns out, other Southern Baptists were not as impressed with Floyd as Hunt was. At the time of his first nomination, Floyd's church gave 0.27 percent of its budget to the Southern Baptist Cooperative Program. This caused the senior pastor of Emmanuel Baptist Church, Mike Stone, to write, 'In thousands of churches this fall, faithful pastors will face skeptical finance committees at budget preparation time. He will go out to bat to keep CP giving strong even in light of building programs and tight budgets. The last thing that warrior needs is for his finance committee chairman to…read that Southern Baptists elected a president whose church gave .27 percent.'"[42] Floyd clearly failed to win

---

[41] The reader should ask himself if an ambitious career-oriented pastor is the kind of shepherd he desires for his family and church.

[42] Dunn, S. (2014, June). *Jared Moore or Ronnie Floyd? 10 Points for Gryffindor*. Retrieved May 16, 2015, from gsethdunn.wordpress.com: https://gsethdunn.wordpress.com/2014/06/06/jared-moore-or-ronnie-floyd-10-points-for-gryffindor/

his first election because he did not to kick-up enough of his mega-church's multi-million dollar revenue to the convention's Cooperative Program. This evidences the existence of a perverse incentive in the Southern Baptist Convention. A pastor's fitness to lead is judged by the amount of money he can raise for the convention. If a pastor wants to be a leader, he is encouraged to adopt a Moses Model, try to get a job at a bigger church, and transfer local control of his church's money to the national convention. This is politicking at its worst. Furthermore, it encourages economically unwise central planning. Local people know how best to spend their own money. The Cooperative Program takes this money out of the hands of local decision makers and passes it through a multi-level bureaucracy stocked with partisans of those at the top. "It all boils down to a simple formula: The extent of misuse is directly proportionate to the distance between the giver and the spender."[43]

---

[43] Branson, M. K. (2007). *Spending God's Money: Extravagance and Misuse in the Name of Ministry.* Lee's Summit, MO: Father's Press, LLC. p.4

Controversies and Mismanagement

"Though we may sometimes be forced to choose between different evils, they remain evils." F. A. Hayek

"Hear the sirens, Hear the circus so profound. I hear the sirens, more & more in this here town" Eddie Vedder

Problems within Southern Baptist entities are legion. In a fallen world, it's simply a fact of life that there will be corruption in any organization. Powerful and wealthy organizations like the SBC are bound to draw individuals who are, at their core, greedy and unChristlike. This unfortunate reality should not completely discourage the creation of cooperative Christian organizations but should cause their participants to be leery of potential of misdeeds: both accidental and purposeful. Some people are just incompetent, not nefarious. It can be hard to tell the difference. In the end, givers to SBC entities can consider definite results even if the motives of offenders' hearts are unknown. The consideration of definite results should include the consideration of accountability. Those who commit misdeeds, whether purposeful or accidental, should be held accountable. Often times, they are not.

Of all the entities of the Southern Baptist Convention, the most egregious one is the Ethics and Religious Liberty Commission. This entity essentially provides culture warriors to see to the political interests of the SBC. Given that, historically, the church has essentially thrived under persecution and that Christians are truly citizens of heaven, there is some question as to whether or not a denominational body should even concern itself with temporal political affairs to the level of having hired lobbyists. In any case, the SBC does so at great expense.

Outspoken pastor Dr. Randy White has decried the ERLC as "a huge waste of money," which has "become (again) a left-leaning social-justice agency of the SBC."[44] To put the spending of the ERLC in perspective, Gospel for Asia could put 8,861 national missionaries on the ground for one year for the amount of money budgeted to the ERLC by the SBC in 2014.[45] Rather than cost-effectively sponsor foreign missions through the IMB or other organizations, the ERLC pays administrative costs for high-paid lobbyists in an expensive city like Washington, D.C. Despite their efforts, "gay marriage" is making inroads in the United States and abortion is still legal and commonplace. In another blunt statement Dave Miller wrote, "I can say that in my 30 years of ministry in Baptist churches, the ERLC (and its predecessor) have made no discernible impact on the work I have done or the churches I have served."[46] Not only are ERLC lobbyists not needed and not cost effective, they seem to be underperforming. To make matters worse, some of the political stances being taken up by the ERLC seem to run against the grain of those of every day Baptists. ERLC president Russell Moore was formerly a staffer for a

---

[44] White, R. (2014, December 28). *Why I'm joining #the15, and I'm not even an angry Calvinist*. Retrieved May 2015, 2015, from Randy White Ministries: http://www.randywhiteministries.org/2014/12/28/ive-joined-the15-im-even-angry-calvinist/#sthash.Msr4jH7X.dpuf

[45] The 2014 ERLC budget was $3.19M according to a Baptist Press article dated September 13, 2013. According to the Gospel for Asia website, an Asian national missionary can be sponsored for $360/year.

[46] Miller, D. (2010, November 2010). *A Great Commission Suggestion: Pink Slip the ERLC*. Retrieved May 16, 2015, from SBC Voices: http://sbcvoices.com/a-great-commission-suggestion-pink-slip-the-erlc/

democratic congressman[47] and has been shown to act like a progressive. While taking up support of a path to citizenship for illegal immigrants, Moore referred to Jesus as an "illegal immigrant".[48] More recently, Moore advised a fellow Christian that he could be supportive of gay loved ones by attending a reception that celebrated a "gay marriage."[49] Unlike most Southern Baptists, the people who actually fund Moore's salary at a grass roots level, Moore comes off as very liberal. For some, Moore is a refreshing change from former long-time ERLC president Richard Land, who resigned among allegations of racial insensitivity and plagiarism.[50] However, although he challenges the status quo, Moore is just a different kind of wrong. He has even hired a different kind of employee at the ERLC; a number of his hires were not even Southern

---

[47] ERLC. (2013, May 30). *Russell Moore: The call to ministry & the public square.* Retrieved MAy 16, 2015, from ERLC.com: http://erlc.com/article/russell-moore-the-call-to-ministry-the-public-square

[48] Moore, R. D. (2011, June 11). *Immigration and the Gospel.* Retrieved May 15, 2015, from RussellMoore.com: http://www.russellmoore.com/2011/06/17/immigration-and-the-gospel/

[49] Dunn, S. (2014, November 3). *Celebrating Sin?* Retrieved May 30, 2015, from Pulpit & Pen: http://pulpitandpen.org/2014/11/03/celebrating-sin/

[50] Kwon, L. (2012, June 1). *So. Baptist Leader Richard Land Reprimanded OVer Traymon Martin Comments.* Retrieved May 30, 2015, from The Christian Post: http://www.christianpost.com/news/so-baptist-richard-land-reprimanded-over-trayvon-martin-comments-75927/

Baptist at the time of their offer of employment with the ERLC.[51]

In April of 2018, Moore's ERLC, in conjunction with The Gospel Coalition, put on a conference in Memphis entitled "MLK50" with the stated purpose of reflecting "on the state of racial unity in the church and the culture"[52] Speakers at the conference included Moore himself, sitting SBC President Steve Gaines, and Danny Akin (the president of Southeastern Baptist Theological Seminary) among others. The timing of the conference was such that it coincided with the 50-year anniversary of the death of revered civil-rights activist Martin Luther King, Jr. King was a Baptist pastor and peaceful voice for equality but also an avowed theological liberal and serial adulterer. Nevertheless an entity of the Southern Baptist Convention named a conference in his honor. In the wake of the MLK50 conference there is a growing concern among Southern Baptists that the Convention is shifting its focus away from the Biblical gospel and towards the social gospel, intersectionality, and cultural Marxism.[53] Southern Baptists who oppose the MLK50 Conference should take their concerns one step further. The ERLC should not exist at all, especially with Russell Moore at its helm. The "ethical" needs of the convention can be fulfilled by

---

[51] Patrick, R. (2014, January 21). *Memo from SBC Headquarters*. Retrieved November 11, 2014, from SBC Voices: http://sbcvoices.com/memo-from-sbc-headquarters/

[52] ERLC/TGC. (2018). *About*. Retrieved June 9, 2018, from MLK50: http://mlk50conference.com/

[53] Buice, J. (2018, June 5). *The SBC at the Intersection of Intersectionality*. Retrieved from Delivered By Grace: http://www.deliveredbygrace.com/the-sbc-at-the-intersection-of-intersectionality/

academics. Seminary ethics and philosophy professors can stake out biblical positions for the denomination. Lobbyists, especially liberal ones, are wasteful and insulting to everyday Southern Baptists. Unfortunately, many every day pew-sitting Baptists do not know that the ERLC exists. If they did, they find might it objectionable for the multiple reasons above explored.

NAMB is much more well known that the ERLC and like the ERLC, it is plagued with controversy. An entire book was written about the financial mismanagement and culture of corruption at the North American Mission Board. That book, *Spending God's Money: Extravagance and Misuse in the Name of Ministry*, was written by former NAMB Director of Marketing Mary Kinney Branson. According to Branson hers is "a rare book."[54] This is because most people who left the North American Mission Board (in the midst of a brewing financial scandal) signed an agreement not to talk or write negatively about the agency or its leaders."[55] This Kinney finds such agreements when undertaken by secular entities to be understandable. What Kinney does not find understandable is "why a Christian agency felt a need to require such a gag document of its employees."[56] During her time at NAMB, Branson "saw firsthand – or heard from reliable sources – of ice sculptures for parties, a business retreat planned around a cruise to the Bahamas, private jets for travel, and millions

---

[54]Branson, M. K. (2007). *Spending God's Money: Extravagance and Misuse in the Name of Ministry.* Lee's Summit, MO: Father's Press, LLC. p.3
[55] ibid
[56] ibid

paid to friends for business not sent out for bids."⁵⁷ Branson ends her book, a recounting of her tumultuous time with NAMB, with the story of the resignation of embattled NAMB President "Hollywood" Bob Reccord. Upon his resignation, which came as scandal over his leadership broke in the Christian press, Reccord received a $500,000 severance package.⁵⁸ On his way out the door, Reccord arranged for a $92,000 payment to be sent to Johnny Hunt (for his Timothy-Barnabas school) and a $300,000 payment to be sent to evangelist Jay Strack."⁵⁹ Both men would later sign a letter vouching for the integrity of Bob Reccord. This letter was signed by thirty-nine other high-profile Southern Baptist leaders, including eight former and future presidents of the convention. (Within the past three years, Hunt invited Reccord to speak at his annual "Johnny Hunt Men's Conference."⁶⁰) All of these men are fairly considered members of the elite SBC

---

⁵⁷ Branson, M. K. (2007). *Spending God's Money: Extravagance and Misuse in the Name of Ministry.* Lee's Summit, MO: Father's Press, LLC. p.5

⁵⁸ Baptist News Global. (2007, March 26). *Church's offering for Reccord raises questions about six-figure severance - See more at: http://baptistnews.com/archives/item/2021-churchs-offering-for-reccord-raises-questions-about-six-figure-severance#sthash.iPYPX4Dj.dpuf.* Retrieved May 16, 2015, from Baptist News Global: http://baptistnews.com/archives/item/2021-churchs-offering-for-reccord-raises-questions-about-six-figure-severance

⁵⁹ Branson, M. K. (2007). *Spending God's Money: Extravagance and Misuse in the Name of Ministry.* Lee's Summit, MO: Father's Press, LLC. p.113

⁶⁰ Dunn, S. (2014, June). *Jared Moore or Ronnie Floyd? 10 Points for Gryffindor.* Retrieved May 16, 2015, from gsethdunn.wordpress.com: https://gsethdunn.wordpress.com/2014/06/06/jared-moore-or-ronnie-floyd-10-points-for-gryffindor/

intelligentsia. While they vouched for Reccord amidst scandals, rank and file NAMB employees were ask to sign confidentiality agreements.

The mismanagement of NAMB does not stop with financial scandal. For example, In Montana NAMB has used funds to plant churches geared specifically toward racecar enthusiasts.[61] Planting churches for a group based upon their hobbies is called the "affinity church model" and it is hardly biblical. In addition to using the affinity church model, NAMB has suggested, among other things, printing the name of one's church on urinal cakes and placing them in the facilities of local bars and taverns as a way of advertising. One NAMB church planter, giving the justification that his son's travel baseball team was "his tribe" and needed to be reached, eschewed Sunday church to travel with his son's baseball team on the weekend. He engaged in this lifestyle while being financially supported by NAMB.[62] Almost certainly there are NAMB missionaries who do faithfully attend and plant sound churches. Yet, there is some question about the oversight of an organization that teaches urinal cake affinity model church growth methods especially when it draws revenue. Giving such advice during church growth and church planting seminars is big business for NAMB (although its marketing department has been considerably reduced since the well-funded days of Branson and Reccord[63]). At these

---

[61] Modern Day Downgrade A Call for Repentance to Southern Baptists and Other Evangelicals.
[62] ibid
[63] As of three years ago the NAMB marketing department consisted of a single person Ashley. I know this from personal experience. Ashley is a schoolmate of mine and an intelligent young woman. She did not contribute an opinion for this document.

Conferences, experts such as John Bisagno advise church planters while offering their own church-growth and management strategy books for sale. NAMB's overall church planting initiative is essentially a Cooperative Program growth tool. Once planted churches take root and grow, like a fast-food franchise, they can begin sending money back to the mother convention (the effective franchisor). Some churches fail and some churches thrive. In denominational church-planting, as is the case with other franchising operations, one has to take risks and spend money to make money. The overall idea of church-planting is certainly great-commission oriented and should not be decried. However, making a policy of planting a churches managed by a denominational employee reflects an Episcopal, and not Baptist, ecclesiology. Local churches should be planted and spun-off from local churches and local people.

A lawsuit has been brought against NAMB by a former denominational employee, Will McRaney, who is calling attention to NAMB's top-down approach. "McRaney is the former Baptist Convention of Maryland/Delaware Executive Director and has long alleged that NAMB interfered with his work at that entity, contributing to the termination of his employment. In a lawsuit he filed against NAMB on April 4th, 2017 McRaney, seeking damages, accuses NAMB of further inference with his ability to earn an income."[64] Outside of the offenses for which McRaney insists NAMB is legally liable, he alleges that current NAMB leadership has "used its financial assets to buy favors, threaten people who raise questions, and undermine

---

[64] Dunn, S. (2017, May 20). *Will McRaney is Suing NAMB and That's Okay*. Retrieved from Pulpit & Pen: http://pulpitandpen.org/2017/05/20/will-mcraney-is-suing-namb-and-thats-okay/

the ministries and careers of leaders who will not 'bow' to its demands, replaced the cooperative spirit characteristic of the previous NAMB (leadership) with strong-arm moves to dominate State Conventions and Associations, and eaten away the cooperative culture built in the SBC over generations."[65] McRaney has also drawn attention to the unusual amount of financial reserves and property that NAMB has accrued. There is some question as to why this money isn't being spent to evangelize the lost. According to McRaney, "While sending some money on to the mission field (current) NAMB (leadership) has kept back large amounts, swelling its 'unrestricted reserves' from $204 million in 2010 when (current) NAMB (leadership) was installed, to about $285 million in 2014. By its operating guidelines, it should only carry $60.5 (1/2 of annual budget) in reserves…Around $62 million has been committed to buy 'houses for church planters' in various states, effectually putting NAMB into the real estate business. Some have questioned if this is actually an attempt to hang onto large amounts of money without it being accounted for as part of the NAMB reserve holdings." The website reformnambnow.org contains a listing of some of the real estate to which McRaney refers, including a $475,000 house in Tucson, Arizona and a $415,000 condo in Alpharetta, Georgia (where NAMB is headquartered).[66] Neither of these properties are in the city limits of a "Send City".

---

[65] McRaney, W. (n.d.). *Is the New NAMB Really Working? – Summary*. Retrieved June 9, 2018, from WillMcRaney.com: http://willmcraney.com/is-the-new-namb-working-summary/

[66] reformnambnow.org. (2018, June). *Property Purchases*. Retrieved from reformnambnow.org: http://www.reformnambnow.org/misuse-of-funds.html#properties

"Send Cities"[67], as designated by NAMB, are ostensibly underserved municipalities. NAMB employees are sent to "Send Cities" to plant churches. These cities are essentially areas in which the SBC has low market share and therefore has room to expand.[68] In response to NAMB's "Send City" initiative, pastor Randy White has written that NAMB should, "fulfill all of its convention assignments, and not be just the large-city church planting agency of the SBC."[69] White may have not considered that there is perhaps more money to be made in the large cities.[70] It should also be remembered that the SBC lost ground in these "send cities"[71] due to the white flight of urban churches to suburbia during the past few decades. According to Bill Leonard, professor of Church history at Wake Forest Divinity School, "Southern Baptists are experiencing such demographic trauma of membership and baptism they need

---

[67] North American Mission Board. (n.d.). *Send Ciites*. Retrieved May 16, 2015, from North American Mission Board: http://www.namb.net/cities/

[68] The Send City program is very similar to an older NAMB program called "Strategic Focus Cities." $14.1 million dollars was directed to the Strategic Focus Cities program in 2006. More information about NAMB activity at that time can be found in a Baptist News Global article located here: https://baptistnews.com/archives/item/948-southern-baptist-missions-suffering-under-nambs-leadership-report-says

[69] White, R. (2014, December 28). *Why I'm joining #the15, and I'm not even an angry Calvinist*. Retrieved May 2015, 2015, from Randy White Ministries: http://www.randywhiteministries.org/2014/12/28/ive-joined-the15-im-even-angry-calvinist/#sthash.Msr4jH7X.dpuf

[70] ibid

[71] This is especially apparent near the city of Atlanta, where I worked for nearly a decade.

new constituencies among nonwhite population."[72] It is arguably this need that is directing NAMB into urban areas. Such an argument is strengthened by the recent activity of the ERLC. Not only has Russell Moore called for a path to citizenship for Hispanic illegal immigrants, the ERLC held a leadership summit on the subject of "The Gospel and Racial Reconciliation" in 2015.[73] Before the well-publicized shooting death of a black suspect by a white police officer in Ferguson, Missouri (a suburb of "Send City" St. Louis Missouri) and the racial rioting that followed, the ERLC summit's planned topic was "Developing a Pro-Life Ethic".[74] It is essential, if Cooperative Program funding levels are to be sustained, for the SBC to increase its membership among minorities, who tend to be more church-going than the non-white population as the overall population of America becomes more secular.[75]

---

[72] Horton, G. &. (2014, May). *Southern Baptists to open their ranks to missionaries who speak in tongues.* Retrieved May 16, 2015, from The Washington Post: http://www.washingtonpost.com/national/religion/southern-baptists-to-open-their-ranks-to-missionaries-who-speak-in-tongues/2015/05/14/1fddd28a-fa7e-11e4-a47c-e56f4db884ed_story.html

[73] ERLC. (n.d.). *Ledership Summit.* Retrieved May 16, 2015, from ERLC.com: https://erlc.com/summit2015

[74] Strode, T. (2015, December 2015). *ERLC Turns to Race Issue for March Summit.* Retrieved May 17, 2015, from Pastors.com: http://pastors.com/erlc-turns-race-issue-march-summit/

[75] Smietana, B. (2014). *Are Millennials Really Leaving the Church? Yes — but Mostly White Millennials* . Retrieved May 17, 2015, from FaithStreet.com: https://www.faithstreet.com/onfaith/2014/05/16/are-

One of the speakers at the ERLC leadership summit on racial reconciliation was Dr. David Uth, the senior pastor of First Baptist Church of Orlando.[76] Uth is one of the forty-one signers of the letter written in support of former NAMB President Bob Reccord.[77] Uth was also a featured speaker at the 2015 Southern Baptist Convention Pastor's Conference.[78] The organizer of the 2015 Pastor's Conference, Willy Rice, faced significant criticism for inviting political pundit and confessed Seventh Day Adventist Ben Carson to speak at the conference.[79] Not only is Carson a member of a Christian cult,[80] he was (for the 2016 election) a Republican candidate for the Presidency of the United States. Carson declared his candidacy shortly after his invitation to speak at the Pastor's Conference was rescinded. According to multiple Baptist objectors, the invitation of a political figure and cult member to speak at the Pastor's Conference was

---

millennials-really-leaving-church-yes-but-mostly-white-millennials/32103

[76] ERLC. (n.d.). *Ledership Summit*. Retrieved May 16, 2015, from ERLC.com: https://erlc.com/summit2015/schedule

[77] Branson, M. K. (2007). *Spending God's Money: Extravagance and Misuse in the Name of Ministry*. Lee's Summit, MO: Father's Press, LLC. p.184

[78] Calvary Church 2014-15. (2015). *About The 2015 SBC Pastors' Conference*. Retrieved May 18, 2015, from SBCPC.com: http://www.sbcpc.net/#speakers

[79] Dunn, S. (2015, May 7). *Ben Carson, the IRS, and an Implicit Rebuke of David Uth and First Baptist Orlando*. Retrieved May 18, 2015, from Pulpit & Pen: http://pulpitandpen.org/2015/05/07/ben-carson-the-irs-and-an-implicit-rebuke-of-jeff-uth-and-first-baptist-orlando/

[80] Seventh Day Adventists believe, among other strange doctrines, that Jesus Christ and the angel Michael are the same person. When considered against Southern Baptist Doctrine, many Seventh Day Adventist beliefs are heretical.

inappropriate. These objections and the rescinding of Carson's invitation were an implicit repudiation of David Uth for his decision to have Ben Carson speak to the congregation of First Baptist Orlando during Sunday services in June 2014.[81] Such a rebuke is rare for a member of the intelligentsia who carries enough clout to be a featured speaker and the Pastor's Conference and the ERLC summit in the same year.

The Pastor's Conference is where the intelligentsia gathers each year before the annual convention begins. The 2015 Pastor's Conference speakers schedule featured the President of the IMB as well as the President of the ERLC. It also featured the current (at the time) SBC President, Ronnie Floyd, who was nominated for another term at the helm of the SBC at the 2015 Southern Baptist Convention by J.D. Greear.[82] Greer was also a Pastor's Conference speaker.[83] (At the 2016 Convention, Greear himself was nominated for the SBC presidency and lost a narrow election to Steve Gaines. Greear won the presidency at the 2018 Southern Baptist Convention in Dallas in a lopsided vote). The Pastor's Conference is effectively a preconvention strategy gathering for the SBC elite.

---

[81] Dunn, S. (2015, May 7). *Ben Carson, the IRS, and an Implicit Rebuke of David Uth and First Baptist Orlando.* Retrieved May 18, 2015, from Pulpit & Pen: http://pulpitandpen.org/2015/05/07/ben-carson-the-irs-and-an-implicit-rebuke-of-jeff-uth-and-first-baptist-orlando/

[82] Baptist Press. (2015, April 20). *Greear to nominate Floyd for 2nd term.* Retrieved May 18, 2015, from Baptist Press: http://www.bpnews.net/44590/greear-to-nominate-floyd-for-2nd-term

[83] Calvary Church 2014-15. (2015). *About The 2015 SBC Pastors' Conference.* Retrieved May 18, 2015, from SBCPC.com: http://www.sbcpc.net/#speakers

Furthermore, it provides a high-profile forum by which the SBC elite can present themselves to the general population of pastors as leaders to be followed. In 1979 the Pastor's Conference was the launching pad for the election of Adrian Rogers to the presidency of the Southern Baptist Convention.[84] Rogers' election was the first step in the decade-long plan, now known as Conservative Resurgence, to eliminate moderates and liberal from the convention. It took power consolidation to make the plan a success. Now, with the moderates and liberals gone, convention influence still seems to remain consolidated in the hands of a small group of SBC intelligentsia. It is important for those who want to direct the Convention to control the Presidency of the SBC because the President appoints the members of the Committee on Committees which in turn nominates the members of the Committee on Nominations which in turn nominates trustees for the boards of the various SBC entities. Conservative Resurgence architect Paul Pressler once remarked, "The lifeblood of the Southern Baptist Convention is the trustees. We need to go for the jugular – we need to go for the trustees."[85] Pressler got them. He perhaps got them a little too well, however. The trustee system is intended to keep entity leadership accountable and in-order. However, trustees do not always act to do such. Former Pressler operative C.B. Scott has remarked that SBC trustees tend to be "boot-lickers" and "bologna sniffers."[86] Trustees, who are often wined and grape-juiced,

---

[84] Hefley, J. C. (1989). *The Truth in Crisis: The Controversy in the Southern Baptist Convention (Vol. 4)*. Hannibal Books p.6

[85] ibid

[86] These adjectives were used by C.B. Scott in a phone conversation with me. We were discussing the weaknesses of trustees at Baptist entities. Scott is a veteran of the Conservative Resurgence.

by charismatic and influential entity heads can lose their objectivity.[87] Those who serve as trustees have the potential to be appointed to high-profile and highly-compensated denominational jobs themselves. Demanding accountability may reduce the chances of their own political success. Given the culture of secrecy and confidentiality agreements in the SBC, it is hard to find public information about the moral hazards of the trustee system.[88] The nature of the Conservative Resurgence demanded strong collusion between entity heads, trustees, denominational officials, and the architects of the resurgence. Unfortunately, ridding the convention of liberals seems to have created a cabal of power brokers who take care of themselves and their own before the conventions best interest. Currently, the convention seems interested in attracting conservative nonwhites. Ben Carson is perhaps the most popular conservative nonwhite in the United States. Intelligentsia members such as David Uth were willing to compromise doctrinal principles for political ones by inviting Carson to one of the most influential events in SBC culture.

The Pastor's Conference "may cost approximately $200,000 to $350,000."[89] These amounts are greater than

---

[87] I am personally reminded of the story of F. Ross Johnson, the former President who essentially tried to "steal the company" using a leveraged buyout. Johnson was an expert in manipulating his board of directors. His story can be found in *Barbarians at the Gate: The Fall of RJR Nabisco* by John Heylar

[88] I do not have at my disposal many published sources to support this argument. I do not, however, make it out of complete ignorance of the trustee culture.

[89] This is according to Dr. Rick Patrick of Southern Baptist Interest group Connect 316. His comments and a discussion around them can be found at

the yearly budgets of many small SBC churches. The use of such amounts of money to produce a conference where pastors preach to other pastors is questionable. Unfortunately, the questionable use of denominational funds for the enjoyment of an anointed few is no uncommon in the SBC arena. Nor is it limited to the national level. Wasteful and questionable spending is apparent in state conventions as well. The palatial headquarters of the Georgia Baptist Convention cost upwards of $42,000,000 dollars to construct. The debt incurred to pay for the construction was eventually paid off using funds formerly designated for medical missions.[90] The ostentatious headquarters of the state convention is a place many pew-sitting Georgia Baptists will never see, yet it is one they fund with their giving. They also fund three colleges. One of the colleges, Brewton-Parker, has been embroiled in financial scandal and other problems for over a decade.[91] It was recently rocked by a race scandal which led to the resignation of its already controversial president, Ergun Caner. The employee who blew the whistle on Caner for his inappropriate action, C.B. Scott was fired and

---

http://sbcvoices.com/breaking-news-sbc-will-survive-carsons-appearance-at-the-pastors-conference/#comment-287672

[90] Dunn, S. (2015, March 19). *Lifestyles of the Rich and Baptist: Creflo Dollar and Robert White.* Retrieved May 18, 2015, from Pulpit & Pen: http://pulpitandpen.org/2015/03/19/lifestyles-of-the-rich-and-baptist-creflo-dollar-and-robert-white/

[91] Dunn, S. (2013, December). *Brewton Parker, Ergun Caner and the Issue of Stewardship: A Georgia Baptist Reaction and Solution by G. Seth Dunn, CPA, MACC.* Retrieved May 18, 2015, from gsethdunn.wordpress.com: https://gsethdunn.wordpress.com/2013/12/16/brewton-parker-ergun-caner-and-the-issue-of-stewardship-a-georgia-baptist-reaction-and-solution-by-g-seth-dunn-cpa-macc/

asked to sign a confidentiality agreement or immediately lose his insurance benefits. The elderly Scott refused as a matter of personal integrity. Had he not done so, another Baptist scandal may have been swept under the rug.[92] Confidentiality agreements were semi-successfully used to sweep a scandal under the rug at Louisiana Baptist College.[93] The story is similar to others in that an embattled entity president, Joe Aguillard in the case of Louisiana College, left his office under suspicious circumstances with a six-figure compensation package.[94] Louisiana College's controlling state convention is so problematic that a new state Baptist association was formed in Louisiana by former college administrator, Tim Johnson. According to Johnson, "There's too much power in the Baptist Building (LBC office in Alexandria) because there's too much money. With the amount of money there, the power's there with it. And that's the problem with our state."[95] One trustee of Louisiana Baptist College, Jay

---

[92] McKissic Sr., W. D. (2015, February 5). *IS A GEORGIA BAPTIST COLLEGE COVERING UP RACISM?* Retrieved May 18, 2015, from dwightmckissic.wordpress.com: https://dwightmckissic.wordpress.com/2015/02/05/is-a-georgia-baptist-college-covering-up-racism/

[93] Allen, B. (2014, February 28). *Documents suggest Louisiana College paid hush money to potential whistleblower - See more at:* https://baptistnews.com/ministry/organizations/item/28411-documents-suggest-louisiana-college-paid-hush-money-to-potential-whistleblower#sthash.imfDPnoV.dpuf. Retrieved May 20, 2015, from Baptist News Global

[94] Reynoso, R. (2014, April 16). *Faith on View.* Retrieved May 20, 2015, from Louisiana College: lies, obfuscation, and a lack of repentance: http://www.faithonview.com/louisiana-college-lies-obfuscation-and-a-lack-of-repentance/

[95] Fryer, K. (2015, 21 January). *LBC PASTORS: "TOO MUCH POWER IN THE BAPTIST BUILDING".* Retrieved May 18,

Adkins, attempted to publically expose the secretive actions of Louisiana College officials which were, arguably, undertaken in order to cover-up the malfeasance that occurred during Aguillard's tenure. However, Adkins achieved limited success and was met with stern resistance from convention insiders. Adkins detailed his trying and compelling story in a series of personal blogs.[96] The Executive Director of the Louisiana Baptist Convention is David Hankins, who co-authored the book One Sacred Effort: The Cooperative Program of Southern Baptists in which he encourages participation in the very Cooperative Program that funds his own scandal-plagued state convention.

On a national educational level, scandals seem to be rarer. The six Southern Baptist seminaries are among the last institutions of theological higher learning in western culture that teach from a high view of scripture.[97] These seminaries, because they exist to train Christian ministers, hold their students to considerably different standards than do secular schools. Most notably, students are expected to be Christians and to live out a Christian lifestyle. However, in 2014, an exception was granted to these standards at Southwestern Baptist Theological seminary. Acting

---

2015, from Pulpit & Pen: http://pulpitandpen.org/2015/01/21/lbc-pastors-too-much-power-in-the-baptist-building/

[96] The story of Jay Adkin's struggle to improve the situation at Louisiana College can be found at his blog, The Crescent Crier.

[97] For the purposes of full disclosure, I do not write from an objective position about SBC seminaries. I attend an SBC seminary and am quite fond of the institution which I attend. I hold to a high view of scripture and naturally favor any institution that teaches from that same view.

unilaterally, Paige Patterson, the co-architect of the Conservative Resurgence the President of that school, admitted a practicing Muslim student into the school's archaeology program.[98] The reaction to this violation of seminary standards was mixed. Some were outraged. Others argued that the matter was a justified form of evangelism.[99] The same pattern of reaction was manifested when Patterson was unceremoniously fired from the presidency of Southwestern in May of 2018. His unequivocal firing came a week after he had been relieved of his duties as President and accepted the title of the seminary's "President Emeritus" and "Theologian in Residence". The details of the controversy surrounding his dismissal are disputed in the media and relate to the propriety of the way he handled allegations of sexual assault on the campuses of Southwestern Baptist Theological Seminary and Southeastern Baptist Theological Seminary (where he formerly served as President). To say the least, the reasons for his firing are questionable.

---

[98] Burleson, W. (2014, May 16). *Istoria Ministries Blog*. Retrieved May 20, 2015, from Southwestern Baptist Islamic Theological Seminary and the Center for Cultural Engagement and Firing: http://www.wadeburleson.org/2014/05/southwestern-baptist-islamic.html

[99] I do not cite specific published documents here but recall my own memories of the various reactions to the Muslim student's enrollment at SWBTS. I spoke with Dr. Patterson about the matter myself; he handled the matter quite gracefully. I personally did not support the enrollment of the non-Christian student, who has now left the school. I did not agree with any of the arguments used to justify the enrollment.

The mixed reactions to the tenure of Paige Patterson at Southwestern provide a perfect example of how the Cooperative Program fails to distribute funding in keeping with the specific concerns of the giver. Rather than distributing money broadly to all seminaries through the Cooperative Program, a giver who disapproved Patterson's admission of a Muslim student could refrain from giving to Southwestern but freely give direct gifts to the other seminaries. Those givers who approved Patterson's admission of a Muslim student could continue to give to his school. The same goes for those who approve or disapprove of the action of the school's trustees of firing Patterson. Direct giving options are available now but many fail to exercise them in deference to the Cooperative Program. For all of the controversies discussed above, there are Southern Baptists on both sides of them. It seems counterintuitive to expect all Baptists to broadly fund controversies to which they object, yet that's exactly what the Cooperative Program is designed to actualize. Those who give to the Cooperative Program, for example, pay to perpetuate the existence of the "Kingdom Diversity" office at Southeastern Theological Seminary. In February of 2018, Southeastern and its Kingdom Diversity Office held "its fifth annual 'African American Read-In.' The event was entitled 'Martin and Malcom' and was advertised as featuring 'the reading of excerpts from and discussion of Martin Luther King Jr.'s *Letter from a Birmingham Jail* and Malcolm X's speech *The Ballot or the Bullet*." [100] If a church is okay with funding such activity, it can

---

[100] Dunn, S. (2018, February 25). *Southern Baptist Seminary Holds MLK and Malcom X "Read-In" Event*. Retrieved from Pulpit & Pen: http://pulpitandpen.org/2018/02/25/southern-baptist-seminary-holds-mlk-malcom-x-read-event/

continue giving to the Cooperative Program or send gifts straight to Southeastern. If a church doesn't want to pay to have students have a Malcom X "read-in" it cease giving to the Cooperative Program and designate its gifts elsewhere.

One option for giving elsewhere is the IMB. Southern Baptists were shocked to learn in 2015 that the IMB was cutting at least 600 missionaries and staff and had spent $210 Million dollars more than it had received over a period of six years.[101] Whether or not the specific spending decisions of the IMB over that time period were wise is a matter for debate. Perhaps the agency was wasteful, perhaps it wasn't. What isn't debatable, however, is that the agency spent more money than it was receiving. This type of spending, over a period of years, is plainly irresponsible. Spending more than one makes doesn't work for families, churches, businesses, or the IMB. Someone must be held responsible. The IMB's spending problem fell into the lap of IMB President David Platt, who took over as the agency's head man in 2014. However, it didn't stay there long as Platt resigned as IMB President in 2018. In the Southern Baptist Convention, IMB missionaries have been brought home from the field while NAMB has purchased real estate and the ERLC has put on conferences. Spending priorities seem to be backwards. Management seems to be in turmoil. Clearly, this is a problem that blind giving to the Cooperative Program is not going to fix. This is a problem, arguably, that blind giving to the Cooperative Program helped create. Unfortunately, most rank and file

---

[101] Smietana, B. (2017, August 17). *Southern Baptists Will Cut 600 to 800 Missionaries and Staff.* Retrieved from Christianity Today: https://www.christianitytoday.com/ct/2015/august-web-only/southern-baptists-will-cut-800-missionaries-imb-david-platt.html

Southern Baptists are probably completely unaware of them.

Big Pastors, Little Churches

"For all our lives the presidents of the SBC have been luminaries and mega-church pastors – celebrities who live in different worlds than we do. They don't really understand how we live and we don't really understand how they live." Dave Miller, former 2nd VP of the SBC

As of 2007, sixty percent of SBC churches had less than 300 members.[102] In order to support their families, the pastors of smaller congregations often have to work a second, secular job in addition to fulfilling their pastoral duties. According to Frank Page, Southern Baptist Executive Committee President, "Some would say 35,000 of our 46,000 churches, maybe more than that, are in the two categories of small church or bivocational."[103] Small-churches are the back-bone and norm of the Southern Baptist Convention. Page has communicated that such churches are the "best way to make disciples in the 21st Century."[104] Yet SBC Presidents are often mega-church pastors with national followings. In the last two decades there has been an almost unbroken chain of mega-church pastors elected to the presidency of the Southern Baptist Convention. The 2014 and 2015 president of the Southern Baptist Convention, Ronnie Floyd, pastors a multi-site

---

[102] Kumer, T. (2007, May 7). *Little People In Little Places: The Average Size Of SBC Churches.* Retrieved April 24, 2015, from Said at Southern: http://saidatsouthern.com/little-people-in-little-places-the-average-size-of-sbc-churches/

[103] Chandler, D. (2014, September 17). *Bivocational church model best, Page says.* Retrieved April 24, 2015, from Baptist Press: http://www.bpnews.net/43375/bivocational-church-model-best-page-says

[104] ibid

mega-church.[105] So, too, do Steve Gaines and JD Greear. Multi-site churches strain the limits of Baptist ecclesiology.[106] Despite their questionable theological appropriateness, they are growing in popularity. According to an article written by LifeWay researcher, Ed Stetzer, at *Christianity Today*, "Among recent church trends, we continue to see multisite churches becoming more and more common. No longer just a new trend, they now number more than 5,000 churches, and growing. Among the 100 Largest churches, we find only 12 have a single campus…On the Fastest-Growing list, the number with a single campus is much greater—42, reflecting close to a split in the number of churches that do and do not have multiple campuses. Multisite is the new normal among large churches and widely embraced elsewhere."[107] Multi-site mega churches and mega preachers are not the norm of the Southern Baptist Convention. Yet mega preachers are commonly elected to lead the convention. The careers of these men are advanced. Their books are sold. Their speaking schedules are booked. They become Christian celebrities. Big Pastors grow rich and famous off of little churches.

The average Southern Baptist pastor is hardly a popular celebrity. The average Southern Baptist pastor is hardly represented by the men who have recently held the presidency of the Southern Baptist Convention. Although

---

[105] In recent years, Floyd's church has removed the word "Baptist" from its name.
[106] But not franchise business models
[107] Stetzer, E. (2014, February 2014). *Multisite Churches are Here, and Here, and Here to Stay*. Retrieved April 24, 2014, from Christianity Today: http://www.christianitytoday.com/edstetzer/2014/february/multisite-churches-are-here-to-stay.html

many of them sit on trustee boards, small church pastors are not a part of the oligarchy of elite power brokers that steer the convention. (They are too busy serving their flocks and trying to make a living.) Given that the Southern Baptist Convention is a democratic organization, it seems strange that obscure small-church pastors would elect multi-site mega preachers to lead their denominational organization. Yet, it appears that they do. A review of Southern Baptist Convention attendance records, however, indicates otherwise. Small church pastors are, by and large, not electing un-relatable mega preachers. In 2004, 8,600 messengers attended the Southern Baptist Convention. At that time there were 43,465 affiliated congregations.[108] That's an attendance rate of less than 20%. Such attendance is likely skewed towards larger church pastors who have the budget to make the expensive trip to whatever city in which the convention is held. In many cases, the pastors of small churches can't afford to go to the convention and don't pay attention to what goes on there. Still, politically disinterested small-churches send in Cooperative Program money to be controlled and distributed by the elite oligarchy. This is terrible stewardship. Millions and millions of Cooperative Program dollars are contributed by churches who put forth little to no effort towards seeing how reasonably it is spent. Small church pastors should stop depending on unchecked bureaucrats to spend their precious mission funds.

---

[108] Brand, C. O. (2009). *One Sacred Effort: The Cooperative Program of Southern Baptists.* B&H Academic p.102

Apathy Among the Laity

"There is an increasing tendency among modern men to imagine themselves ethical because they have delegated their vices to larger and larger groups." Reinhold Niebuhr

"Rather than useful jobs in our country, people have been offered bureaucratic 'make work,' rather than moral leadership, they have been given bread and circuses, spectacles, and, yes, they have even been given scandals. Tonight there is violence in our streets, corruption in our highest offices, aimlessness among our youth, anxiety among our elders and there is a virtual despair among the many who look beyond material success for the inner meaning of their lives. Where examples of morality should be set, the opposite is seen. Small men, seeking great wealth or power, have too often and too long turned even the highest levels of public service into mere personal opportunity." Barry Goldwater

Congregants in church pews are perhaps even less engaged than their pastors when it comes to being aware and concerned about how the SBC operates and spends Cooperative Program funds. The money that funds the state and national SBC network doesn't just come from local churches, it comes from the pockets of pew-sitting Christians. In the American church, the pew is fast becoming indistinguishable from the theater seat. Both church music and preaching is becoming more and more entertainment-driven and less and less spiritually challenging. Preachers can draw cheers by preaching politically palatable (and profitable) sermons that never convict congregants of sin. This entertainment-driven and consumerist environment is an outworking of a seeker-sensitive mindset. Priority is placed on getting lost people in the door and not upsetting them too much where they'll leave. Under this culture of revivalism, the evangelical movement has "cast aside an older model of leaders as holy men and instead (given) rise to leaders who (are) entrepreneurs – pragmatic marketers who (are) willing to use whatever (works) to get conversion."[109] The revivalistic seeker-sensitive mindset persists because personal evangelism rates among the laity are shamefully low. "Only half (52%) of born again Christians say they actually did share the Gospel at least once this past year to someone with different beliefs, in the hope that they might accept Jesus Christ as their Savior."[110] Low personal evangelism rates are consistent with the "invest-and-invite" model that has been modeled by Baptist churches in recent decades.

Congregants give. Churches build buildings. Congregants invite "seekers" to hear evangelistic messages given in big buildings by paid professional preachers. Evangelism and missions, like many other tasks in the American economy, are outsourced to hired guns. The SBC is perhaps the biggest hired gun in Christendom. Apathetic and disengaged pew-sitters hire-out their great commission responsibilities at state, national, and international levels by giving to money to the Cooperative Program through their local church. Without knowing to what and to whom they are giving, apathetic laypeople fund a largely unaccountable denominational bureaucracy. Baptist laypeople should stop depending on unchecked bureaucrats to spend their precious mission funds. It's almost

---

[109]Pearcy, N. (2004). *Total Truth: Liberating Christianity from Its Cultural Captivity.* Crossway Books p. 286

[110] Barna Group. (2013). *Is Evangelism Going Out of Style?* Retrieved April 24, 2015, from Barna Group: https://www.barna.org/barna-update/faith-spirituality/648-is-evangelism-going-out-of-style#.VTsLOCHBzRY

inexplicable that many every day Baptists are fed up with a massive, unaccountable federal government that taxes heavily and spends irresponsibly and contrary to their ideals but do next to nothing to exact denominational leaders to the same degree of scrutiny with which they examine the federal government.

Stewardship and Ecclesiology

"We've all heard it hundreds of times—SBC Headquarters is the local church and not some denominational agency. If this line is nothing more than a misleading notion humbly tossed out under the pretense of sounding spiritual, then we should stop saying things we do not really mean." Rick Patrick[111]

Church members are obligated to support their local congregations. However, their ecclesiastical fiscal responsibility stops there. There is absolutely no scriptural prescription for giving to the Cooperative Program or any other denominational cause. There is a biblical mandate for good stewardship, however. Since all local Baptist churches are autonomous, church members have the right and responsibility to consider whether or not it is a good stewardship to give undesignated funds to the Cooperative Program. Such funds will be spent at the discretion of convention leadership or a denominational agency. Despite the protests that may come from denominationally indoctrinated pastors, it is not the responsible of a Southern Baptist church to give away money to relic of 1920s era progressivism, especially when the information age makes giving directly to a specific cause so much easier than it was to do in the 1920s.

Despite any misconceptions to the contrary, a church does is not required to give to the Cooperative Program in order to be considered Southern Baptist. "A church is Southern Baptist by definition if it participates with the Southern Baptist Convention in at least one of the following ways:

---

[111] Patrick, R. (2014, January 21). *Memo from SBC Headquarters.* Retrieved November 11, 2014, from SBC Today: http://sbcvoices.com/memo-from-sbc-headquarters/

(1) gives to the Cooperative Program; (2) gives to the Lottie Moon Offering, IMB directly; (3) gives to the Annie Armstrong Offering, NAMB, directly; (4) is dually aligned with the SBC; (5) is a member of a local SBC Association; or (6) gives to the SBC Executive Board directly."[112] Giving to a local SBC association, for example, qualifies a church as "Southern Baptist". Its ministers are therefore eligible for Guidestone participation and its members are therefore eligible for discounted tuition at a Southern Baptist seminary. Giving locally and directly not only qualifies a church to be a part of the SBC, it is conducive to better stewardship. Receivers of local and directly given money are inherently more accountable.

---

[112] My source on this is a church endorsement form from a Southern Baptist Seminary.

Giving Around the Cooperative Program

"We shall not grow wiser before we learn that much that we have done was very foolish." F. A. Hayek[113]

No program is needed to facilitate giving to Baptist causes; any SBC entity will gladly accept a check from any church or individual person. Mission board websites allow for on-line giving to specific programs (printing Bibles, buying meals in Africa, disaster relief, etc...) Seminaries have scholarship programs by which individuals can sponsor individual students. An individual person can simply write a check to a seminary student (or school, or professor) they know and trust. In fact, he can write a check to any needy person without the need for a national program to pass the money through three levels of bureaucracy. International Missionaries are now available to Skype live from the mission field with the local churches that support them. A local church does not need to go through IMB to support and interact with a foreign missionary. The internet lists countless Baptist church plants that need support; money does not need to be passed through NAMB to get it to them.[114] If someone was so inclined, he could even give money to the ERLC political cause. If churches favor giving generally to entities such as the IMB, they can. Churches who operate under unfavorable state conventions can give around them by giving straight to national causes. Churches who prefer their state and local conventions can give designated funds to those organizations.

---

[113] Hayek, F. A. (1972). *The Road to Serfdom.* Chicago: University of Chicago Press.

[114] While their IMB counterparts are generally able to depend on salaries paid by IMB, NAMB missionaries are largely expected to raise their own personal financial support.

Direct giving is, at its core, free-market giving. Giving through the Cooperative Program is essentially like asking one's church to ask the state convention to ask the national convention to go to the grocery store to buy his groceries. It would be more efficient if he went to the store himself and bought his own groceries. He would get exactly what he wanted. He would know exactly what everything costs. He would think about what he was spending. Direct giving engenders better stewardship because the giver has to consider the merits of the cause to which he is giving. The direct giver sees every cent and can hold the receiver directly accountable…as God will surely hold him accountable.

There is no need to continue to engage in Cooperative Program giving, it is tantamount to Baptist socialism. It has a caused enough ills. It's time for fiscally social conservative Baptists to pull their money and that of their churches out of the pockets of the mega preachers and denominational elites. These men have, for far too long, have bestrode the narrow Baptist world like a colossus. Their multisite churches are growing beyond control at a rate similar to the bloated United States government. Their political machinations are more concerned with earthly kingdoms than heavenly ones. Those who continue to financially support them are on a road to serfdom. It's time for those people to come off of it by implementing direct giving.

Those who do so may face stern opposition from those who have been long-time supporters of the Cooperative Program. "When Friedrich Hayek's *The Road to Serfdom* attacked the welfare state and socialism in 1944, he characterized his adversaries as 'single-minded idealists' and 'authors whose sincerity and disinterestedness are above suspicion,' but his own book was treated as something immoral…"[115] There are many good, well-intentioned Baptists who, to their own folly, support the Cooperative Program. Speaking at a press conference, the first SBC President of the Conservative Resurgence, Adrian Rogers, remarked that Southern Baptists "have made a golden calf of the (Cooperative) program…It's almost easier to be against the Virgin Birth than the program."[116] Pastors and lay people who advocate giving around the Cooperative Program should be prepared to face stern resistance from those who are faced with melting down their long-time idol and drinking a bitter elixir made from its ashes.

---

[115] Sowell, T. (1995). *The Vision of the Annointed*. Basic Books p.3

[116] Shurden, W. B. (1996). *Going for the Jugular: A Documentary History of the SBC Holy War*. Mercer University Press.

Bibliography

Allen, B. (2014, February 28). *Documents suggest Louisiana College paid hush money to potential whistleblower - See more at: https://baptistnews.com/ministry/organizations/item/28411-documents-suggest-louisiana-college-paid-hush-money-to-potential-whistleblower#sthash.imfDPnoV.dpuf.* Retrieved May 20, 2015, from Baptist News Global: https://baptistnews.com/ministry/organizations/item/28411-documents-suggest-louisiana-college-paid-hush-money-to-potential-whistleblower

Baptist News Global. (2007, March 26). *Church's offering for Reccord raises questions about six-figure severance - See more at: http://baptistnews.com/archives/item/2021-churchs-offering-for-reccord-raises-questions-about-six-figure-severance#sthash.iPYPX4Dj.dpuf.* Retrieved May 16, 2015, from Baptist News Global: http://baptistnews.com/archives/item/2021-churchs-offering-for-reccord-raises-questions-about-six-figure-severance

Baptist Press. (2015, April 20). *Greear to nominate Floyd for 2nd term.* Retrieved May 18, 2015, from Baptist Press: http://www.bpnews.net/44590/greear-to-nominate-floyd-for-2nd-term

Baptist Studies Online. (2007, February). *Original Constitution of the Southern Baptist Convention.* Retrieved November 30, 2014, from http://baptiststudiesonline.com/: http://baptiststudiesonline.com/wp-content/uploads/2007/02/constitution-of-the-sbc.pdf

Barna Group. (2013). *Is Evangelism Going Out of Style?* Retrieved April 24, 2015, from Barna Group: https://www.barna.org/barna-update/faith-spirituality/648-is-evangelism-going-out-of-style#.VTsL0CHBzRY

Bisagno, J. R. (2011). *Pastor's Handbook n* (Kindle Edition ed.). B&H Publishing.

Brand, C. O. (2009). *One Sacred Effort: The Cooperative Program of Southern Baptists.* B&H Academic.

Branson, M. K. (2007). *Spending God's Money: Extravagance and Misuse in the Name of Ministry.* Lee's Summit, MO: Father's Press, LLC.

Buice, J. (2018, June 5). *The SBC at the Intersection of Intersectionality.* Retrieved from Delivered By Grace: http://www.deliveredbygrace.com/the-sbc-at-the-intersection-of-intersectionality/

Burleson, W. (2014, May 16). *Istoria Ministries Blog.* Retrieved May 20, 2015, from Southwestern Baptist Islamic Theological Seminary and the Center for Cultural Engagement and Firing: http://www.wadeburleson.org/2014/05/southwestern-baptist-islamic.html

Calvary Church 2014-15. (2015). *About The 2015 SBC Pastors' Conference.* Retrieved May 18, 2015, from SBCPC.com: http://www.sbcpc.net/#speakers

Chandler, D. (2014, September 17). *Bivocational church model best, Page says.* Retrieved April 24, 2015, from Baptist Press: http://www.bpnews.net/43375/bivocational-church-model-best-page-says

Cumings, B. (2009). *Dominion from Sea to Sea: Pacific Ascendancy and American Power.* Yale University Press.

Dunn, S. (2013, December). *Brewton Parker, Ergun Caner and the Issue of Stewardship: A Georgia Baptist Reaction and Solution by G. Seth Dunn, CPA, MACC.* Retrieved May 18, 2015, from gsethdunn.wordpress.com: https://gsethdunn.wordpress.com/2013/12/16/brewt

on-parker-ergun-caner-and-the-issue-of-stewardship-a-georgia-baptist-reaction-and-solution-by-g-seth-dunn-cpa-macc/

Dunn, S. (2014, November 3). *Celebrating Sin?* Retrieved May 30, 2015, from Pulpit & Pen: http://pulpitandpen.org/2014/11/03/celebrating-sin/

Dunn, S. (2014, June). *Jared Moore or Ronnie Floyd? 10 Points for Gryffindor.* Retrieved May 16, 2015, from gsethdunn.wordpress.com: https://gsethdunn.wordpress.com/2014/06/06/jared-moore-or-ronnie-floyd-10-points-for-gryffindor/

Dunn, S. (2015, May 7). *Ben Carson, the IRS, and an Implicit Rebuke of David Uth and First Baptist Orlando.* Retrieved May 18, 2015, from Pulpit & Pen: http://pulpitandpen.org/2015/05/07/ben-carson-the-irs-and-an-implicit-rebuke-of-jeff-uth-and-first-baptist-orlando/

Dunn, S. (2015, March 19). *Lifestyles of the Rich and Baptist: Creflo Dollar and Robert White.* Retrieved May 18, 2015, from Pulpit & Pen: http://pulpitandpen.org/2015/03/19/lifestyles-of-the-rich-and-baptist-creflo-dollar-and-robert-white/

Dunn, S. (2017, May 20). *Will McRaney is Suing NAMB and That's Okay.* Retrieved from Pulpit and Pen: http://pulpitandpen.org/2017/05/20/will-mcraney-is-suing-namb-and-thats-okay/

Dunn, S. (2018, February 25). *Southern Baptist Seminary Holds MLK and Malcom X "Read-In" Event.* Retrieved from Pulpit & Pen: http://pulpitandpen.org/2018/02/25/southern-baptist-seminary-holds-mlk-malcom-x-read-event/

Elliot, H. (2007, November 27). *Georgia Baptist resolution criticizes Baptist blogs.* Retrieved May 16, 2015, from Baptist Standard Publishing: https://www.baptiststandard.com/resources/archives

/47-2007-archives/7247-georgia-baptist-resolution-criticizes-baptist-blogs

ERLC. (2013, May 30). *Russell Moore: The call to ministry & the public square.* Retrieved MAy 16, 2015, from ERLC.com: http://erlc.com/article/russell-moore-the-call-to-ministry-the-public-square

ERLC. (n.d.). *Ledership Summit.* Retrieved May 16, 2015, from ERLC.com: https://erlc.com/summit2015

ERLC/TGC. (2018). *About.* Retrieved June 9, 2018, from MLK50: http://mlk50conference.com/

Fryer, K. (2015, 21 January). *LBC PASTORS: "TOO MUCH POWER IN THE BAPTIST BUILDING".* Retrieved May 18, 2015, from pulpitandpen.org: http://pulpitandpen.org/2015/01/21/lbc-pastors-too-much-power-in-the-baptist-building/

Georgia Bapist Convention. (2013). *We Believe In the Cooperative Program.* Retrieved May 22, 2015, from Georgia Bapist Convention: http://gabaptist.org/we-believe-in-cp/

Greenspan, A. (2008). *The Age of Turbulence: Adventures in a New World.* Penguin.

Hayek, F. A. (1972). *The Road to Serfdom.* Chicago: University of Chicago Press.

Hefley, J. C. (1989). *The Truth in Crisis: The Controversy in the Southern Baptist Convention (Vol. 4).* Hannibal Books.

Horton, G. &. (2014, May). *Southern Baptists to open their ranks to missionaries who speak in tongues.* Retrieved May 16, 2015, from The Washington Post: http://www.washingtonpost.com/national/religion/southern-baptists-to-open-their-ranks-to-missionaries-who-speak-in-tongues/2015/05/14/1fddd28a-fa7e-11e4-a47c-e56f4db884ed_story.html

IMB. (2015). *Fast facts*. Retrieved May 28, 2015, from www.imb.org: http://www.imb.org/1307.aspx#.VWer0PlVhBc

James, S. (2015, MAy 7). *What Not to Do When a Fellow Christian Embarrases Us*. Retrieved May 16, 2015, from Patheos.com: http://www.patheos.com/blogs/inklingations/2015/05/07/what-not-to-do-when-a-fellow-christian-embarrasses-the-rest-of-us/

Kumer, T. (2007, May 7). *Little People In Little Places: The Average Size Of SBC Churches*. Retrieved April 24, 2015, from Said at Southern: http://saidatsouthern.com/little-people-in-little-places-the-average-size-of-sbc-churches/

Kwon, L. (2012, June 1). *So. Baptist Leader Richard Land Reprimanded Over Traymon Martin Comments*. Retrieved May 30, 2015, from The Christian Post: http://www.christianpost.com/news/so-baptist-richard-land-reprimanded-over-trayvon-martin-comments-75927/

Malphurs, A. (2003-09-01). *Being Leaders: The Nature of Authentic Christian Leadership* (Kindle Edition ed.). Baker Publishing Group.

McKissic Sr., W. D. (2015, February 5). *IS A GEORGIA BAPTIST COLLEGE COVERING UP RACISM?* Retrieved May 18, 2015, from dwightmckissic.wordpress.com: https://dwightmckissic.wordpress.com/2015/02/05/is-a-georgia-baptist-college-covering-up-racism/

McRaney, W. (n.d.). *Is the New NAMB Really Working? – Summary*. Retrieved June 9, 2018, from WillMcRaney.com: http://willmcraney.com/is-the-new-namb-working-summary/

Miller, D. (2010, November 2010). *A Great Commission Suggestion: Pink Slip the ERLC*. Retrieved May 16,

2015, from SBC Voices: http://sbcvoices.com/a-great-commission-suggestion-pink-slip-the-erlc/

Miller, D. (2015, May 8). *"Dave Miller for President" and Other Dumb Ideas!* Retrieved May 16, 2015, from SBC Voices: http://sbcvoices.com/dave-miller-for-president-and-other-dumb-ideas/

Modern Day Downgrade A Call for Repentance to Southern Baptists and Other Evangelicals. (n.d.). Retrieved May 16, 2015, from https://www.youtube.com/watch?v=AJW6Y69sIC0

Moore, R. D. (2011, June 11). *Immigration and the Gospel.* Retrieved May 15, 2015, from RussellMoore.com: http://www.russellmoore.com/2011/06/17/immigration-and-the-gospel/

NAMB. (2015). **2015 NORTH AMERICAN MISSION BOARD MINISTRY REPORT.* Retrieved May 28, 2015, from www.namb.net: http://www.namb.net/annualreport/

North American Mission Board. (n.d.). *Send Ciites.* Retrieved May 16, 2015, from North American Mission Board: http://www.namb.net/cities/

Patrick, R. (2014, January 21). *Memo from SBC Headquarters.* Retrieved November 11, 2014, from SBC Voices: http://sbcvoices.com/memo-from-sbc-headquarters/

Pearcy, N. (2004). *Total Truth: Liberating Christianity from Its Cultural Captivity.* Crossway Books.

reformnambnow.org. (2018, June). *Property Purchases.* Retrieved from reformnambnow.org: http://www.reformnambnow.org/misuse-of-funds.html#properties

Reynoso, R. (2014, April 16). *Faith on View.* Retrieved May 20, 2015, from Louisiana College: lies, obfuscation, and a lack of repentance: http://www.faithonview.com/louisiana-college-lies-obfuscation-and-a-lack-of-repentance/

Shellnutt, K. (2018, May 30). *Paige Patterson Fired by Southwestern, Stripped of Retirement Benefits*. Retrieved from Christianity Today: https://www.christianitytoday.com/news/2018/may/paige-patterson-fired-southwestern-baptist-seminary-sbc.html

Shurden, W. B. (1996). *Going for the Jugular: A Documentary History of the SBC Holy War*. Mercer University Press.

Smietana, B. (2014). *Are Millennials Really Leaving the Church? Yes — but Mostly White Millennials*. Retrieved May 17, 2015, from FaithStreet.com: https://www.faithstreet.com/onfaith/2014/05/16/are-millennials-really-leaving-church-yes-but-mostly-white-millennials/32103

Smietana, B. (2017, August 17). *Southern Baptists Will Cut 600 to 800 Missionaries and Staff*. Retrieved from Christianity Today: https://www.christianitytoday.com/ct/2015/august-web-only/southern-baptists-will-cut-800-missionaries-imb-david-platt.html

Sowell, T. (1995). *The Vision of the Annointed*. Basic Books.

Sowell, T. (2008, December 23). *Another Great Depression?*. Retrieved November 2014, 30, from NationalReview.com: http://www.nationalreview.com/articles/226599/another-great-depression/thomas-sowell/page/0/1

Stetzer, E. (2014, February 2014). *Multisite Churches are Here, and Here, and Here to Stay*. Retrieved April 24, 2014, from Christianity Today: http://www.christianitytoday.com/edstetzer/2014/february/multisite-churches-are-here-to-stay.html

Strode, T. (2013, September 13). *TRUSTEES: ERLC budget set at $3.19M*. Retrieved May 28, 2015, from Baptist Press:

http://www.bpnews.net/41089/trustees-erlc-budget-set-at-319m

Strode, T. (2015, December 2015). *ERLC Turns to Race Issue for March Summit*. Retrieved May 17, 2015, from Pastors.com: http://pastors.com/erlc-turns-race-issue-march-summit/

White, R. (2014, December 28). *Why I'm joining #the15, and I'm not even an angry Calvinist*. Retrieved May 2015, 2015, from Randy White Ministries: http://www.randywhiteministries.org/2014/12/28/ive-joined-the15-im-even-angry-calvinist/#sthash.Msr4jH7X.dpuf

Appendix 1

2014 National House Vote by Religion

% of each religious group who reported voting Democratic or Republican in the race for the U.S. House of Representatives in their district

	2006		2010		2014	
	Dem	Rep	Dem	Rep	Dem	Rep
Protestant/other Christian	44	54	38	59	37	61
White Prot./other Christian	37	61	28	69	26	72
Catholic	55	44	44	54	45	54
White Catholic	50	49	39	59	38	60
Jewish	87	12	n/a	n/a	66	33
Something else	71	25	74	24	67	31
None	74	22	68	30	69	29
White evangelical/born-again	28	70	19	77	20	78
All others	60	38	55	42	55	43

Note: Throughout this report, "Protestant" refers to people who described themselves as "Protestant," "Mormon" or "other Christian" in exit polls; this categorization most closely approximates the exit poll data reported immediately after the elections by media sources. In this report, some estimates for previous years might differ slightly from previous Pew Research Center analyses due to differences in data coding. Data on Jewish voters in 2010 are not included due to insufficient sample size.

Source: National Election Pool national exit polls. 2014 data from NBC News.

PEW RESEARCH CENTER

Appendix 2

1924 Presidential Election Map

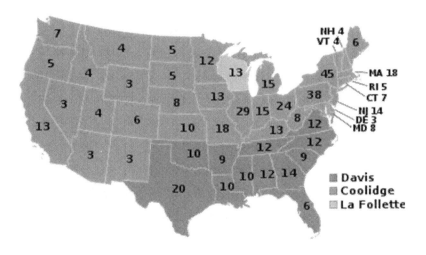

1928 Presidential Election Map

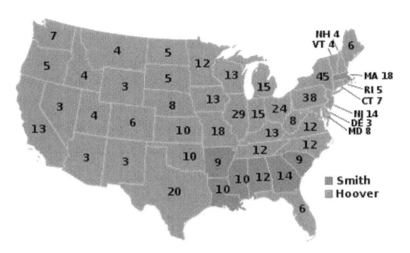

1932 Presidential Election Map

1936 Presidential Election Map

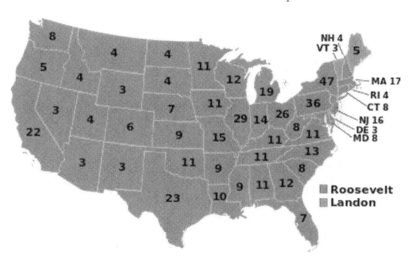

1940 Presidential Election Map

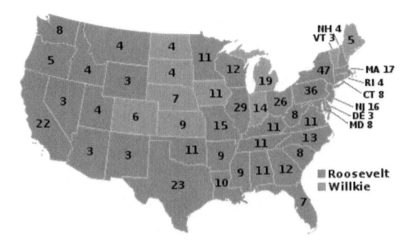

Made in the USA
Lexington, KY
08 August 2018